DEALING WITH
SPIRITUAL
DEFILEMENT
Dr. D.K. Olukoya

Dealing
With
Spiritual
DEFILEMENT

Dr. D.K Olukoya

Dealing with Spiritual Defilement

Published - July 2011

ISBN 978-978-8424-95-6

Published by The Battle Cry Christian Ministries
322, Herbert Macaulay Way, Yaba
P. O. Box 12272, Ikeja, Lagos.
Website: www.battlecryng.com
Phone: 2348033044239, 01-80444415

I salute my wonderful wife, pastor Shade, for her invaluable
support in the ministry

I appreciate her unquantifiable support in the book ministry as the cover designer, art editor
and art adviser.

All Scripture is from the King James Version
Cover illustration: Sister Shade Olukoya

Dr. D.K Olukoya

Dr. D.K Olukoya

CONTENTS

The devil has prepared a lot of evil vitamins and tonic that a lot of people swallow everyday. There are varieties of evil food that people eat every time and they are not aware that they are eating a demonic junk. That is why the Bible makes it clear that you can feed yourself from the table of God and you can also feed yourself from the table of the devil.

What is food?
Food is a nutrition. Food means nourishment. Food gives support. Food is when you sustain something. Anything that is used as nourishment is called food. When you eat something you absorb it into the body. After you have eating the food, You now digest it into the body system.

When you eat, you partake of something. When you eat you take in something. To eat, you comply and cooperate with something. To eat is to receive something joyfully and with enthusiasm. To eat is to believe without questioning.

Therefore, to eat something is to incorporate it into your personality and it becomes part of you. When you put food into your mouth and you chew it, and digest it, it will enter into your body and it will become part of you.

The first food sacrificed to idols that many men eat all over the world is the food of entertainments.

People can sit down and be entertained by television for several hours. What they see and hear on the television set are being swallowed and digested. They watch entertainment until it becomes part and parcel of them. As a believer, you will never make a success of the Christian race until you spend time in prayer. Until you spend quality time waiting on the Lord, until you spend quality time meditating on the scripture you will never succeed as a believer.

A lot of people spend their time reading unprofitable magazines. When you watch video films for good three hours and do not sleep when it is necessary to do so and but you now feel sleepy when it comes to prayer, then something has been programmed into your life.

A lot of people go to cinemas to watch films and they go back home loaded with different kinds of demons from which they washed in their body. A lot of people listen to the music of the world in the name of entertainment when such is actually a food that is sacrificed to idols.

The truth is that the greatest witchcraft in the world is the television and not the blood sucking demons.

When you buy a television set, you place it at the centre of your room where everybody who comes in to your room will see it. It is a conspicuously sitting altar because it is positioned where people will want to see it. You will know the power of television when there is any football competition. People's eyes will be glued to the television and they will even ignore church services for football matches relayed through the television. This is act of drinking from an evil well and it is causing trouble all over the world.

Let us consider the major meals served on the devil's dining table.

1. **Television has been taken over by lust:** All you need to do is to put the television on, you will see an array of programmes sponsored by lust. There are covetousness, violence and witchcraft on television sets. The message the enemy is using the television to pass across to the people bothers on food sacrificed to idols. If you must watch the television set, watch what is essential. It should not be indiscriminate. Neither should it be an all-day affair.

2. **Partying:** Partying means abandoning yourself to fun. If you love parties, you are eating food sacrificed to idols. When somebody celebrates a birthday party three times in a year and you attend, unknown to you they party is for a spiritual exchange.

3. **Alcohol:** The Bible makes it clear that all the prophets of God should abstain from alcohol. The enemy has designed a lot of techniques by adding alcohol to sweets, chocolates and people buy them out of ignorance. The Bible says separation to God includes abstinence from alcohol. You cannot take a cup of beer and say you want to go for night vigil. All the faculties in your body must be intact before you can resist the attack of the enemy. It is a fact that alcohol is a weapon that household wickedness use to hinder destiny. drop of alcohol in your mouth charges your system. Medically, alcohol can destroy the brain cells. A Christian must never do anything that will defile his body. All over the world, the commonest method of inducing demonic joy or demonic gratification is alcohol consumption. The prophets of God were banned from drinking. If you don't drink beer or dry gin and you take palm wine you are still taking an alcohol.

There are particular tribes in this country that are slaves to palm wine. Such people need deliverance from foundational palm wine demons.

4.   **Drugs:** Hard drugs are satanic meals. There are people who use all kinds of drug. There are people who employ drugs to get into the spirit realm. Some people take drugs to release their brain tention temporarily. It is difficult to imagine Jesus Christ coming to the pulpit influenced by drugs. All drugs, tobacco, cigarettes and alcohol will mess up the temple of the Lord whom you are. They are food sacrificed to idols. Evil spirits are always happy seeing a lot of people eating food sacrificed to idols.

5.   **Inordinate desire for money:** The way some people run after money is simply alarming. The worst crime is caused by the desire to acquire money. A lot of women are lost because of money. No one can serve God and money. You have to choose one out of the two. Every inordinate pursuit of money is part of the food sacrificed on idols agenda. It is a tragedy for you to trade your salvation for money.

Money is a general food that the whole world is feeding from. Yet, it is a food sacrificed to idols.

6.   **Love for luxuries:** When you are addicted to luxury, you are eating a demonic meals.

7.   **Ambition for power:** Greed for power makes you a slave at the demonic table.

All of these food sacrificed to idols have destroyed so many lives and have put the whole world into bondage. The Bible says:

> *Ye cannot drink the cup of the Lord, and the cup of devils: ye cannot be partakers of the Lord's table, and of the table of devils.* 1Corinthians 10:21.

The Bible makes it clear that the devil has a table just as God has a table. The question is, from whose table are you feeding yourself? Whatever you eat from the devil you will vomit. It will give you stomach ache and you will regret ever eating from the devil's table.

The devil feeds people with both slow and fast poison. It may take ten years for victims of slow poison to manifest. It may take ten years for the devil's poisonous food to manifest. So many people are regularly feeding on the devil's table. This explains why heaviness and pain are felt after eating in the dream. Have you not wondered in your heart that all these roadside sacrifices you see, who feeds on them? The Bible makes us to understand that doing things at a crossroad is sacrificing foods to the devil. The Bible says:

> For the king of Babylon stood at the parting of the way, at the head of the two ways, to use divination: he made his arrows bright, he consulted with images, he looked in the liver. Ezekiel 21:21.

The Lord forbids participation on the table of the devil. If you feed on that table you are in trouble. When you notice that you are overcome by a religious spirit and you no longer feel the touch of God, you no longer hear God and no sermon of God can change you, you commit sin without being troubled at all. When you experience bad dreams and negative visions. It is the evidence that you are feeding on the devil's table.

Have you been to a place where satanic tongues spoke and others claim to interprete it, then you have fed from the devil's table? Do you have occult books in your house? Have you received a magazine containing demonic pictures? then you have eaten from the devil's table. Perhaps you have gone to visit a fetish priest, there is no way you will visit a witch doctor and remain the same. You would have been infected by their demonic powers.

Have you purchased charms or have you licked charms before, you have fed from the devil's table. Have you swallowed concoctions and incisions all in the name of protection? You have fed from the devil's table.

When you pray very vigorously and you notice something moving around your body it means you have fed from the devil's table. If you do not notice any movement in your body it means you have not prayed the way you should pray. If you pray and you invoke the fire of God into your body, any strange thing or food you have eaten from the devil's table will be exposed and be destroyed.

When you call yourself a born again Christian and you still have a serious lust in your heart, you have eaten the food sacrificed to idols. The Bible says:

> *The children gather wood, and the fathers kindle the fire, and the women knead their dough, to make cakes to the queen of heaven, and to pour out drink offerings unto other gods, that they may provoke me to anger.*
> Jeremiah 7:18.

When you feed on food like honey, oil, alligator pepper on a child's dedication day, you are just feeding on foods sacrificed to idols.

The enemy has worked hard on the black man. He has spent much time working on the black man. This is the reason why they blackman cannot be easily delivered from the bondage of the enemy.

I used to have a friend who travelled to America and came back as a pastor to Nigeria. He thought that American style of preaching would work here. He forgot that the forefathers of the Americans were the ones who introduced Christianity, while his own forefathers were buried in idol worship. He was invited to preach in a cathedral and all of a sudden the Holy Spirit told him to tell the members of the congregation to release whatever form of charms they had on them. At first, he did not believe it, but when he passed across the word of knowledge to the congregation he was amazed at the way people were throwing charms to the pulpit.

From that day, he changed his style of preaching and praying. Some people were born into the midst of witches and wizards and immediately, their stars were stolen. Those are the people the enemy will quickly feed on its table.

There are instances where people have been saved food and when they came back to check the food they found the food as turned to wood or stones. Most people who are fighting against terrible spirits today got into trouble through food. They drank anointing oil and holy water from the wrong places.

At this point, pray this prayer:
Any evil food that is hiding in my body, planning to manifest later, dry up, in the name of Jesus.

Beloved, you have to go back to the Lord's table and leave the devil's table. You need to challenge your system. You need to challenge your spirit. You need to challenge your life with the fire of God so that fire can expose whatever food that was sacrificed to idols that you have eaten from the devil's table. Once the fire of God enters your life, the serpents in your life will jump out and your life will not remain the same again.

PRAYER POINTS

1. My stomach, receive the fire of God, in the name of Jesus.

2. Every food that I have eaten from the table of darkness, dry up, in the name of Jesus.

3. Every demoting food that I have eaten as a child, die, in the name of Jesus.

4. Satanic concoction in my body, die, in the name of Jesus.

5. Every power constructing a coffin for me, die, in the name of Jesus.

6. Every eternal enemy arresting my progress, your time is up, die, in the name of Jesus.

7. Satanic dinning table of my father's house, scatter, in the name of Jesus.

8. My head, reject the arrows of death, in the name of Jesus.

CHAPTER TWO

DEALING WITH SPIRITUAL DEFILEMENT

THE TRAGEDY OF SPIRITUAL DEFILEMENT

Defilement is a very serious subject in the Bible. It is a subject we do not even hear too much about, but it is a very important subject.

What is defilement? How does someone get defiled? Let us read the verse below

> *But Daniel purposed in his heart that he would not defile himself with the portion of the king's meat, nor with the wine which he drank: therefore he requested of the prince of the eunuchs that he might not defile himself. Daniel 1:8.*

From the above passage we discover that Daniel purposed in his heart that he will not defile himself. This is why we read so many beautiful testimonies about Daniel in the Bible. He understood the tragedy of defilement and decided that he will never allow himself to be defiled.
Daniel and his three other colleagues were taken to a

20

foreign land and they could have decided to defile themselves without anybody questioning them but they did not. The truth about Babylon is that all the food served in the king's palace were first of all dedicated to Babylon's idols. So Daniel knew that if he continued eating their food, he would be defiled.

Despite the fact that these four boys were under pressure to copy Babylonian lifestyle, they refused. They wanted to remain pure. It is true that nobody in life wants to be a misfit but sometimes trying not to be a misfit can be very bad.

If you take a cursory look at Eagles, you will observe that they do not fly in a flock. It is true that it is not easy to remain a lone ranger.

The Bible makes us to know that we are a peculiar people and as such we should remain pure. When they discovered that despite the fact that they put so much pressure on the young boys they decided to change their names. The first person was called Annaniah which means God is gracious, they changed his name to Shedrach which means command of Aku which is an idol in Babylon. The second boy's name was Mechile which means who is like God? they changed his name to Meshach meaning who is like unto Aku their idol. The third child was Hazaria which means the Lord has helped me. They changed his name to Abednego meaning servant of Nego which is also an idol in Babylon. The fourth boy's name was Daniel meaning God is my judge. They changed it to Beltheshazar meaning may Balak the idol protect us. However the text retained his name as Daniel.

The man decided that he was born a Daniel and he would die a Daniel. No wonder many of the powerful revelations which we read about came from Daniel. Because Daniel purposed in his heart that he would not defile his heart.

The environment we are presently living in was neutral. It has no problems. It is we human beings living in it that has polluted it. This means it is possible to defile a land. Defilement can be made possible through a lot of factors.

(For all these abominations have the men of the land done, which were before you, and the land is defiled;) That the land spue not you out also, when ye defile it, as it spued out the nations that were before you. Leviticus 18:27-28.

When men continue to defile the land a time will come when the land would spit out such a person. This is what we sometimes fail to understand.

Defile not therefore the land which ye shall inhabit, wherein I dwell: for I the LORD dwell among the children of Israel. Number 35:34.

Every human being is a potential desecrator of land. You can defile anything you lay your hands upon if you are not careful. If you continue to defile the place a time will come when it would spit you out.

*Lift up thine eyes unto the high places,
and see where thou hast not been lien
with. In the ways hast thou sat for them,
as the Arabian in the wilderness; and
thou hast polluted the land with thy
whoredoms and with thy wickedness.
Therefore the showers have been
withholden, and there hath been no
latter rain; and thou hadst a whore's
forehead, thou refusedst to be ashamed.*
Jeremiah 3:2-3.

If you come from a polygamous home certainly that house where all the women live is a polluted house. If you live in an area where all kinds of immorality goes on then you are living in a defiled environment.

Defilement is a serious subject in the Bible.

*Having therefore these promises,
dearly beloved, let us cleanse ourselves
from all filthiness of the flesh and spirit,*

24

perfecting holiness in the fear of God. 2
Corinthians 7:1.

You can defile your flesh and you can also defile your spirit.

Every time there is defilement the Almighty gets angry.

> *Know ye not that ye are the temple of God, and that the Spirit of God dwelleth in you? If any man defile the temple of God, him shall God destroy; for the temple of God is holy, which temple ye are.* 1Corinthians 3:16-17.

The passage makes us to know that if you defile the temple of God which is your body, what follows is destruction.

> And what agreement hath the temple of God with idols? for ye are the temple of the living God; as God hath said, I will dwell in them, and walk in them; and I will be their God, and they shall be my people. 2 Corinthians 6:16.

Know ye not that your bodies are the members of Christ? shall I then take the members of Christ, and make them the members of an harlot? God forbid. What? know ye not that he which is joined to an harlot is one body? for two, saith he, shall be one flesh. But he that is joined unto the Lord is one spirit. Flee fornication. Every sin that a man doeth is without the body; but he that committeth fornication sinneth against his own body. 1Cornthians 6:15-18.

Immediately you sleep with a man or woman outside your marriage, you join to be one flesh. The implication of this is that, if the person you slept with is a witch or wizard you automatically become a witch or wizard. You are not only sharing in sex, you are also sharing in the demons of your partner.

Every time defilement happens, the Almighty gets very angry. Your body, soul and spirit can be defiled. Your properties can be defiled. Your children can be defiled.

Your destiny can be defiled. So many things can suffer defilement.

Defilement means to violate, to contaminate and to corrupt something. To defile also means to deflower, to degrade and make something unclean. It also means to pollute, to poison and to devalue.

Defilement chases away good things from people. You need to understand that this has hindered so many people from being blessed. Some people pray hot prayers but their problems seem to multiply. Some even command the Heavens to open, but it seems that the more they command, the more Heaven get tightly closed.

Some people have done multiple deliverance but no breakthrough. Some would have positive dreams but negative reports. Defilement is the opposite of being kept pure and holy. The Bible makes us to understand the agents of defilement. These agents of defilement shall be examined in the next chapter.

27

CHAPTER THREE

DEALING WITH AGENTS OF DEFILEMENT

There are about fifteen agents of defilement. Unfortunately defilement has no respect for age. Neither does it have respect for your status.

Once defilement sets in, the Almighty gets angry and then destruction sets in. This is why we need to be very careful with what we do with our bodies.

1.   **The first agent of defilement is following the way of unbelievers**

> *Defile not ye yourselves in any of these things: for in all these the nations are defiled which I cast out before you:* Leviticus 18:24.

Trying to copy the world and unbelievers would bring defilement into your life. Once you can stand up and confidently say you have decided to follow Jesus, your life is separated from defilement.

2.   Seeking after wizards and agent s of darkness.

> *Regard not them that have familiar*
> *spirits, neither seek after wizards, to be*
> *defiled by them: I am the Lord your*
> *God.* Leviticus 19:31.

When you go to the agents of darkness for help of any form, you are engaged in a primitive trade by barter with the enemy.

3.   The third agent of defilement is abortion.

> *And I will set my face against that man,*
> *and will cut him off from among his*
> *people; because he hath given of his*
> *seed unto Molech, to defile my*
> *sanctuary, and to profane my holy*
> *name.* Leviticus 20:3.

All those who are killing babies in the womb are giving their seed unto Molech. It will pollute and defile their lives.

4.   Making and serving idols.

*Then said I unto them, Cast ye away
every man the abominations of his eyes,
and defile not yourselves with the idols
of Egypt: I am the LORD your God.*
Ezekiel 20:17.

All form of idolatory is defilement. There are so many
problems the black man has but if you ask me to tell you the
one that has dragged the black man back very fast, I will tell
you it is idolatory. Anywhere there is idolatory there is
serious backwardness. I pray that any shackle of idolatory
holding you to a stagnant position shall be broken in the
name of Jesus.

This is why we keep telling people at the Mountain of Fire
and Miracles Ministries that there are certain names that
God can never write in the book of life. God cannot write a
name like Sangowawa in the book of life. God cannot write
Ogunseyi. God is against idolatory and therefore would not

take his pen and write Sango in His own book. Making and serving idols is an instrument of defilement. I decree that anyone making idolatory to cage you from afar will fail in the name of Jesus.

5.   The fifth form of defilement is shedding of blood

> *For your hands are defiled with blood, and your fingers with iniquity; your lips have spoken lies, your tongue hath muttered perverseness.* Isaiah 59:3.

Anytime the human blood is shed (particularly, innocent blood) there is always a defilement. There is no head of government anywhere, since the beginning of history ,that has been busy killing people and ends up well. Generally they end up being killed, either physically or spiritually.

6.   Evil food.

> *But I say, that the things which the Gentiles sacrifice, they sacrifice to*

*devils, and not to God: and I would not
that ye should have fellowship with
devils.* 1Corinthians 10:20.

When you eat polluted food it defiles you. All these
spiritually dedicated food that is being served in worldly
parties would defile you.

7.   The seventh agent of pollution is the mouth.

*And the tongue is a fire, a world of
iniquity: so is the tongue among our
members, that it defileth the whole
body, and setteth on fire the course of
nature; and it is set on fire of hell.*
James 3:6.

The tongue which is that large muscle inside the mouth can
defile the whole body. Your mouth can release poison into
your life. Your mouth can destroy your destiny, completely.
Each word you speak without allowing the Holy Ghost to
purify it before you speak would defile you. Many of us

need to padlock our mouths so that we can stop defiling our bodies.

8.   Death can defile.

All the abortions will produce defilement or death. Hospital and clinics are sometimes being defiled because of the kind of things they sometimes do there. Any action carried out which produces death will defile.

9.   The ninth agent of defilement is evil spitting.

10.   Sexual impurity.

This has destroyed the world to an unimaginable level. Both young men and ladies have been destroyed and are still being destroyed.

> *Marriage is honourable in all, and the bed undefiled: but whoremongers and adulterers God will judge.* Hebrews 13:4.

Sexual impurity defiles and these include inordinate

affections, foolish fondness, unlawful sexual intercourse, prostitution, unlawful cohabitation, lesbianism, homo-sexualisms, raping, pornography, lust and all evil sexual appetite. Incest is another terrible thing which involves having sex with either your father, daughter or blood relation.

The Bible tells us that any form of incest puts the person and his descendants under a curse up till their tenth generations. Incest means you are trying to look at the nakedness of your family members either in secret or through the bathroom door. This is what Ham did in the Bible and the repercaution are still here with us. All kinds of very terrible things follow incest.

11.   Medical defilement.
Stuffing yourself with poison and using of herbs with questionable origin can put you under defilement. If you have to go to the hospital that is not run by Christians you may have to pray on everything they are putting on you or in your body.

12. The twelfth agent of defilement is mutilation of the body.

All the cutting, marking, tattooing, piercing, disfiguring of the body which is common now is defiling the temple of God. By piercing your skin you open the doors of your life to agents for invasion and blood hunters. If you draw anything on your body you are defiling your body and there might be no pastor to help you when it backfires.

> *Ye shall not make any cuttings in your flesh for the dead, nor print any marks upon you: I am the LORD.* Leviticus 19: 28.

As far as the Bible is concerned piercing of ears is not allowed. Tribal marks on your face are not allowed. Incisions are not allowed. They are all agents of defilement.

13. Drugs.

There are many dangers that one gets exposed to after the use of drugs. There are many demons attached to the use of drugs. There is a spirit called the spirit of sorcery. It works with drugs. So, you have to be careful with the kind of drugs you take.

14.   Cursed materials in the house.
If you have a cursed material in the house, it would defile the house and it would cause trouble.

15.   Invasion by astral bodies.
Some human beings have the power to leave their bodies and enter into another person's body. They will then infilterate the life of the person. This is the fifteenth thing that can defile.

SYMPTOMS OF DEFILEMENT
When a person is being defiled, God in His mercy sometimes opens your eyes. In your dreams you would begin to have the dreams of defilement where you see yourself naked in the dream. You would also find yourself among excreta or you find yourself locked out of the church.

You could see yourself wearing rags or even having sex in the dream or somebody spits on you. Once you are having these dreams the Almighty is telling you that there is defilement. When there is defilement in the body, the glory of God cannot fill that life. The person would continue to be a second hand Christian, demons would continue to pay the person visits, the presence of God would not be able to rest on that life because it would be dirty, the anointing of God would not work upon that life and sickness would be so common to that life once the defilement is not removed. Another symtoms is the tragedy of a person praying the wrong prayers or doing the wrong things.

DEALING WITH DEFILEMENT
What do you do to get out of defilement?
1. **Carry out a spiritual research on your life.** Know who you are, where you are coming from, the kind of things you have involved yourself in, the kind of women or men you have slept with. Review your life. Review whether you have inherited anything that is putting you in trouble now.

38

2. **You need genuine repentance**: Promise God that you will not go back to the life of defilement.

3. **Forgive those who have offended you**. As far as you nurse bitterness in your heart the bitterness would bring you more defilement.

4. **Break every ungodly soul-tie**. You have to review the kind of friends you have or have had and break any unfodly soul-tie.

5. Cast out the evil spirits and the effects of those terrible relationships on your life. You need deliverance.

6. Ask God to cleanse your life.

7. Ask God to reverse any consequence of what the enemy has left behind in you body. This is important.

A lot of people have entered into bondage and are going from bondage to bondage because they never really dealt with spiritual defilement. Some have consumed the food of defilement which was what Daniel avoided which made his dreams to be cleaned and his revelations were accurate.

You must deal with spiritual defilement today.

CHAPTER FOUR

TAKING GOD SERIOUSLY

And there came two angels to Sodom at even;
and Lot sat in the gate of Sodom: and Lot
seeing them rose up to meet them; and he
bowed himself with his face toward the
ground; And he said, Behold now, my lords,
turn in, I pray you, into your servant's house,
and tarry all night, and wash your feet, and ye
shall rise up early, and go on your ways. And
they said, Nay; but we will abide in the street
all night. And he pressed upon them greatly;
and they turned in unto him, and entered into
his house; and he made them a feast, and did
bake unleavened bread, and they did eat. But
before they lay down, the men of the city, even
the men of Sodom, compassed the house
round, both old and young, all the people from
every quarter: And they called unto Lot, and
said unto him, Where are the men which came
in to thee this night? bring them out unto us,
that we may know them. And Lot went out at
the door unto them, and shut the door after
him, And said, I pray you, brethren, do not so

wickedly. Behold now, I have two daughters which have not known man; let me, I pray you, bring them out unto you, and do ye to them as is good in your eyes: only unto these men do nothing; for therefore came they under the shadow of my roof. And they said, Stand back. And they said again, This one fellow came in to sojourn, and he will needs be a judge: now will we deal worse with thee, than with them. And they pressed sore upon the man, even Lot, and came near to break the door. But the men put forth their hand, and pulled Lot into the house to them, and shut to the door. And they smote the men that were at the door of the house with blindness, both small and great: so that they wearied themselves to find the door. And the men said unto Lot, Hast thou here any besides? son in law, and thy sons, and thy daughters, and whatsoever thou hast in the city, bring them out of this place: For we will destroy this place, because the cry of them is waxen great before the face of the LORD; and the LORD hath sent us to destroy it. And Lot went out, and spake unto his sons in law, which married his daughters, and said, Up, get you out of this place; for the LORD will destroy this city. But he seemed as one that mocked unto his sons in law. And when the morning arose, then the angels hastened Lot, saying, Arise, take thy wife, and thy two daughters, which are here; lest thou be consumed in the iniquity of the city. And while he lingered, the men laid hold upon his hand, and upon the hand of his wife, and upon the hand of his two daughters; the LORD being merciful unto him: and they brought him forth, and set him without the city. And it came to pass, when they had brought them forth abroad, that he said, Escape for thy life; look not behind thee, neither stay thou in all the plain; escape to the mountain, lest thou be consumed. And Lot said unto them, Oh, not so, my Lord: Behold now, thy servant hath found grace in thy sight, and thou hast magnified thy *mercy, which thou hast shewed unto me in saving my life; and I cannot escape to the mountain, lest some evil take me, and I die: Behold now, this city is near to flee unto, and it is a little one: Oh, let me escape thither, (is it not a little one?) and my soul shall live. And he said unto him, See, I have accepted thee concerning this thing also, that I will not overthrow this city, for the which thou hast spoken. Haste thee, escape thither; for I cannot do any thing till thou be come thither. Therefore the name of the city was called Zoar. The sun was risen.upon the earth when Lot entered into Zoar. Then the LORD rained upon Sodom and upon Gomorrah brimstone and fire from the LORD out of heaven; And he overthrew those cities, and all the plain, and all the inhabitants of the cities, and that which grew upon the ground. But his wife looked back from behind him, and she became a pillar of salt. And Abraham gat up early in the morning to the place where he stood before the LORD: And he looked toward Sodom and Gomorrah, and toward all the land of the plain, and beheld, and, lo, the smoke of the country went up as the smoke of a furnace. And it came to pass, when God destroyed the cities of the plain, that God remembered Abraham, and sent Lot out of the midst of the overthrow, when he overthrew the cities in the which Lot dwelt. And Lot went up out of Zoar, and dwelt in the mountain, and his two daughters with him; for he feared to dwell in Zoar: and he dwelt in a cave, he and his two daughters. And the firstborn said unto the younger, Our father is old, and there is not a man in the earth to come in unto us after the manner of all the earth: Come, let us make our father drink wine, and we will lie with him, that we may preserve seed of our father. And they made their father drink wine that night: and the firstborn went in, and lay with her father; and he perceived not when she lay down, nor when she arose. And it came to pass*

46

on the morrow, that the firstborn said unto the younger, Behold, I lay yesternight with my father: let us make him drink wine this night also; and go thou in, and lie with him, that we may preserve seed of our Father. And they made their father drink wine that night also: and the younger arose, and lay with him; and he perceived not when she lay down, nor when she arose. Thus were both the daughters of Lot with child by their father. And the firstborn bare a son, and called his name Moab: the same is the father of the Moabites unto this day. And the younger, she also bare a son, and called his name Benammi: the same is the father of the children of Ammon unto this day. Gen 19:1-38.

The book of Genesis is filled with lamentable and tragic occurrences. Genesis chapter 19 paints a very terrible picture of life in a place called Sodom and Gomorrah. The city is a symbol of open and shameless perversion. Even in Genesis 19:4, the Bible says:

*But before they lay down, the men of the city,
even the men of Sodom, compassed the house
round, both old and young, all the people from
every quarter:* Gen 19:4.

THE EXPIRY DATE

This verse tells us that some visitors came from heaven to
visit a person and the men of the city wanted to mess them
up sexually. Both old and young and even all the people of
Sodom were perverse people. The city was over populated
with strange human beings. Men from this city were
involved in all kinds of sexual activities. God had been
watching the city for a while. God gave them a very long
rope but God had an expiry date. Once He gets tired of what
you are doing, then trouble starts. The Bible says:

*And the LORD said, Because the cry of Sodom
and Gomorrah is great, and because their sin
is very grievous.* Gen 18:20.

The verdict of God was very clear. Because for every sin
that you commit, a voice is there to cry to heaven. The cry of

the sins of Sodom and Gomorrah was so loud in heaven that God arose to deal with the city. Lot and his family were drawn to Sodom, his family live among this perverse people. No doubt the ways and acts of the people of Sodom and Gomorrah became what the Lot family emulated. But God clearly wanted Lot's deliverance and He announced a very clear evacuation plan for Lot. The Bible says:

> *And when the morning arose, then the angels hastened Lot, saying, Arise, take thy wife, and thy two daughters, which are here; lest thou be consumed in the iniquity of the city. And while he lingered, the men laid hold upon his hand, and upon the hand of his wife, and upon the hand of his two daughters; the LORD being merciful unto him: and they brought him forth, and set him without the city. And it came to pass, when they had brought them forth abroad, that he said, Escape for thy life; look not behind thee, neither stay thou in all the plain; escape to the mountain, lest thou be consumed. Gen 19:15-17.*

THE BACKSLIDER

The Bible makes it clear that God gave Lot a clear warning to run for his life or else he would be consumed by the wrath of the Lord. He was told never to look back and never to stop moving because the doom of Sodom and Gomorrah was imminent. The Lord rained fire and brimstone on the city and the corrupt city sank slowly as the waters of the dead sea covered Lot and his family. Only the legs of the wife were running but her heart was not running. The Bible says;

> *But his wife looked back from behind him, and she became a pillar of salt.* Gen 19:26.

Lot's wife went straight to hell from Sodom. She lagged behind. She looked back. Why was she staying behind? Because she was still attached to Sodom and Gomorrah. She wilfully refused to cut off her emotional ties to that city.

Beloved, pulling away from sin may be very difficult. Sin has an attraction for the flesh. The people of Sodom and

Gomorrah were not taking God seriously when they heard that the city was going to be destroyed. But, when it happened, the mocking became screams of terror and death. What killed Lot's wife? What did Jesus say in Luke chapter 17:32?

Remember Lot's wife. Luke 17:32.

Lot's wife died because she saw no need to take God seriously. She knew what God was saying and she rejected it. That was why she perished with her name, although she was a wife of a righteous man. She made a good start but she did not finish well. Lot's wife died in the hands of the angel trying to save her life.

BEWARE

A lot of people are not taking God seriously. If you don't like what your pastor is saying and you don't believe in the doctrine but please take God seriously because if you don't take Him seriously you can end up perishing like Lot's wife did. She heard what the Lord said but she did not take it seriously and it cost her her life.

A REVELATION

I remember a woman who died and was to be buried by her daughter. During her life, she was a high-class prostitute who used to jump from one man to the other. When she died, her daughter came from abroad with fancy clothes and make up to bury her mother. She dressed her mother with fancy clothes, made her hair and even painted her lips. When I got to the place, I asked her why she was dressed that way. The daughter said she wanted her mother to be fancied by the time she got to heaven. But I told her that her mother had arrived at hell even before she died. She was surprised and looked at me with a stunned silence.

The daughter on the night before the burial, had a dream that the trumpet sounded and people were flying; even the fattest person was flying. She noticed she was not flying. She tried to fly but she landed back on the floor and she saw her mother beside her. Both of them were not flying.

HEAVEN OR HELL

God has been showing people who love Him from their hearts how the end will be. If you have been living a carefree life like the people of Sodom and Gomorrah then you will perish. Death is the king of all. It cannot be avoided. But the question is when you die where will you be? When you leave this planet will you leave a footprint that people will remember you to be a child of God? The important thing about death is not death itself, but what follows after death.

There are so many people that God speak to their heart about what to do and what not to do but they are not taking God seriously. God has called some people to work on their behaviour but they refuse to listen to God. People go to church but they don't take God seriously. There are only two ways to die; either in the Lord or outside the Lord. It is either you are saved or you are not saved. It is either you are a child of God or you are a child of Satan. It is either you are headed for heaven or hell. There is no middle camp. It is either you die as a forsaken sinner or as a forgiven saint. Whether you like it or not, if the rapture does not happen, death will surely come.

DEATH IS INEVITABLE

One day, a professor whose wife had been waiting upon the Lord for a baby for sixteen years, was in the lecture room the day they brought the news to him that his wife delivered a baby. He jumped up with joy and by the time he landed on the floor. He was dead. Here was a professor who was teaching in the morning. He never knew he will die in the afternoon of that same day. Death is inevitable. Death has no respect for anointing. The Bible says;

Now Elisha was fallen sick of his sickness whereof he died. And Joash the king of Israel came down unto him, and wept over his face, and said, O my father, my father, the chariot of Israel, and the horsemen thereof. 2 Kings 13:14

Elisha, the man with a double portion of anointing died. Later his dead dried bones raised the dead but he still died. Death is no respecter of holiness. The Bible says;

54

And Samuel died; and all the Israelites were gathered together, and lamented him, and buried him in his house at Ramah. And David arose, and went down to the wilderness of Paran. 1 Sam 25:1

Samuel was the man that heard the voice of the Lord at a young age. Moses never fell sick for one day yet he died. Death can take the old and the young. Death can wait and take the person when he is old. Death does not forget anybody. It has no respect for age, career or your education. Death killed Solomon with all his wisdom. It killed the rich and the poor. Therefore, it is very important at any point in your life to obey God seriously. Brethren, obey God seriously.

A SOBER TRUTH

One sober solemn truth that all preachers face is that, in spite of many people they have preached the gospel to, some will still go to hell fire. A day is coming, which is a day of fear and anger. The day of destruction, the day of the ungodly. It is a day of testing to all mankind. A day which shall burn as an oven. Because God shall blow His final whistle just as He blew His final whistle on Sodom and Gomorrah. The scripture in the book of Revelation 6:17 will come to pass. The Bible says:

> *For the great day of his wrath is come; and who shall be able to stand?* Rev 6:17.

The evil you are hiding will become public knowledge. There will be many men and women from different countries that will be there. The Jews will be there, the Gentiles will be there. Nations where gospel of the Lord has reached or has not reached will be there.

All nationalities and all the people that have passed away will be there. Those who have died will all rise. The dead shall rise from their graves. Those who died in unknown lands will come out. The earth which we place our feet that is gradually turning to a massive graveyard, will release all those who are buried in the ground. Every man born of a woman shall come out from the prolific womb of the earth.

TWO GROUPS

The sea shall release all those who perish in it. Multitudes upon multitudes shall be gathered before this great judge. What a gathering this will be! The Lord will sit on His throne and He will judge. He will divide everyone into two groups. The sheep and the goat. The goat who did not allow the word of God to break their horns will be gathered in the camp of goats. The rebellious goats who do not hear the word of the Lord including the goatish ushers, the goatish singers will face judgement.

The goatish people will be gathered in the great goats camp. The people who rebelled against God will be gathered as goats. It is only the sheep that God has business with. That is why the Bible calls Jesus Christ the lamb of the world.

It is the goatish Christians who disobey the word of God. The wife of Lot was a very senior goat indeed. She saw the angels of the Lord and she refused all the instructions given to her. Yet, her heart was still attached to the world.

EXAMINE YOURSELF

When you are attached to the world and the world sinks, definitely, you will sink with the world. When you call yourself a Christian and the way you dress, your outlook, character and behaviour is not different from the world, then you will be qualified as a goat.

Here in lies the great thought, when this division takes place, where will you be? Has iniquity left your heart? Has rebellion left your life? Is your heart really right with God? You got to church but have you really met God?

You go to the house of God, but are you part of the solution or the problem? Are you really broken in your heart? Are you really on fire for God? Are you the kind of person who pollutes the house of God? You have to obey God seriously.

A COSTLY MISTAKE

There was a couple who wanted to get married in a church. The man of God decided to solemnise them. But during the quiet time, God told him not to solemnise the couple because they were not children of God. But the man of God refused to listen to God because the couple have paid him some money. God told him to return the money to the couple. The pastor argued with God and God decided to let him be.

On the wedding day, the pastor had an accident on his way to the church to solemnise the couple. He lost his two legs to the accident and he spent the rest of his life on the wheel chair all because he did not obey God.

The young prophet in the Bible made a mistake by praying for Jeroboam who was against God.

WAGES OF DISOBEDIENCE
There was a pastor who prayed for a king who was always blaspheming God. One day he blasphemed God and one of the servants of God spoke paralysis into his life and the king's right hand and leg got paralysed. Another pastor who wanted fame, was called to pray for the king for healing. God warned the pastor not to pray for the king but because he wanted fame and popularity, he did not listen to God. On a Saturday he went and prayed for the king but because God's name is a credible name, the king got healed. But on

59

Monday, the deliverance pastor died because he did not obey God.

The Bible said there shall be two positions, the right hand for the sheep and the left hand for the goat. There will be no third position. You are either for God or for satan. There are only two people in the world. Those who are dead in their sins and those who are alive for God. You are either spiritually alive or dead.

You need to pray that the goatish spirit must depart from your life. If you allow the goatish spirit, it will waste your destiny. The eye of fire will read your heart and the hypocrite will have no place to hide. There is a judge that nobody can bribe, He will judge according to your deeds. His tribunal can never be avoided. Once the separation of the sheep from the goat is done, no linking bridge, no crossing over and no hope of restoration. The separation is irreversible.

SPIRITUAL LETHARGY

Nowadays, people don't take God seriously. The spiritual deadness is so high that sinners jump into the presence of God with no concrete conscience. When people get born again with the Bible salvation there will be a change in such people's life. Then their lives will be re-arranged.

Beloved, you cannot hide your sins successfully, Your sin will expose you and single you out. There will be a pay day one day. Your sin will take you farther than you want to go has sin will put you into hell fire. But if you are obeying the totality of the word of God and you are broken in your spirit, then ninety percent of your spiritual warfare is over.

Hell is a lake of fire. Hell is a black knight of infinite darkness. Hell is a place that is on fire forever. Hell is a terrible place whereas Heaven is a beautiful place where no night can overshadow anyone. The Lord is looking for people who want to seperate the goatish spirit out of their lives. The Lord is looking for people who are not rebellious. If you don't obey your pastor, obey God, because there are enough signs that the world is coming to an end.

REPENT!

When you know that the spiritual fire you have is completely gone, and you know that the love your heart has for God is lost; You know God has been speaking to your heart but you ignore Him. You know that the tablet of your heart is polluted by all kinds of worldly things. When you know you practise sexual perversion. When you know you are not right with God. You have to cast out shame and go on your knees and tell God to have mercy on you.

Tell God to forgive you and renew your vows with the Lord. If you do not obey God, it is better you pray to God for forgiveness and renew your position with Him. God is looking for those He can penetrate into their hearts. It will be a tragedy, if heaven cannot connect you and you cannot connect heaven. You must obey God. If His eyes of mercy are shut there is no way out for you. You must repent from your evil deeds and remember Lot's wife. You must tell God to heal you from your evil deeds and lust for the world. You must reconstruct your life.

Prayer Points:

1. Every agent of defilement in my life die, in the name of Jesus.
2. I pull out the messenger of satan for my body by fire, in the name of Jesus.
3. Every evil power asign to posses me, you are lier, die in the name of Jesus.
4. Anything in my life that chases God away, my Father remove it, in the name of Jesus.
5. My Father make me to climb higher, make me dig deeper into your life for me, in the name of Jesus.
6. Every area of my life, that needs to be broken, Holy Ghost break them down, in the name of Jesus.
7. Oh heavens, visit my dream life, in the name of Jesus.

Other Publication by Dr. D.K Olukoya

DEALING WITH SPIRITUAL DEFILEMENT

Defilement is a very serious subject in the Bible therefore, it is important to know what defilement can do and the havoc it can cause.

A life can be defiled. Also, it is possible to defile a land or an environment. Once defilement is in place, there will be little or no progress.

Defilement chases away good things because anytime there is defilement, the Almighty gets very angry.

There are certain heights you can never achieve physically and spiritually no matter how hard you work or struggle once you are defiled. Multiple deliverances cannot help except defilement is identified and addressed. This book takes a holistic look at this subject. Therein you find the sources, dangers and consequences of defilement and how to deliver yourself so that you can be totally free.

A careful study of this book will promote your life.

ABOUT THE AUTHOR

Dr. D. K. Olukoya is the General Overseer of the Mountain of Fire and Miracles Ministries and The Battle Cry Christian Ministries.

The Mountain of Fire and Miracles Ministries' Headquarters is the largest single Christian Congregation in Africa with attendance over 120,000 in single meetings.

MFM is a full gospel ministry devoted to the revival of apostolic signs, Holy Ghost Fireworks, miracle and the unlimited demonstration of the power of God to deliver to the uttermost. Absolute holiness within and without as spiritual insecticide and pre-requisite for heaven is openly taught. MFM is a do-it-yourself Gospel Ministry, where your hands are trained to wage war and your fingers to do battle

Dr. D. K. Olukoya holds first class honours degree in micro biology from the University of Lagos and the PhD in molecular genetics from the University Of Reading, United Kingdom. As a researcher, He has over Seventy Scientific publications to his credit.

Anointed by God, Dr. D. K. Olukoya is a Prophet, evangelist, teacher and preacher of the word. His life and that of his wife, Shade and their Son Elijah Toluwani are living proofs that all power belongs to God.

www.ingramcontent.com/pod-product-compliance
Lightning Source LLC
Chambersburg PA
CBHW062030040426
42447CB00010B/2220